T0113666

Know Your *Worth*

Far More Precious Than Rubies

Nancy Wimberly

WESTBOW
PRESS®
A DIVISION OF THOMAS NELSON
& ZONDERVAN

WestBow Press books may be ordered through
booksellers or by contacting:

WestBow Press
A Division of Thomas Nelson & Zondervan
1663 Liberty Drive
Bloomington, IN 47403
www.westbowpress.com
1 (866) 928-1240

Scripture quotations taken from The Holy Bible, New International
Version® NIV® Copyright © 1973 1978 1984 2011 by Biblica,
Inc. TM. Used by permission. All rights reserved worldwide.

Scripture taken from the King James Version of the Bible.

ISBN: 978-1-9736-9796-1 (sc)
ISBN: 978-1-9736-9797-8 (e)

Library of Congress Control Number: 2020913438

Print information available on the last page.

WestBow Press rev. date: 08/13/2020

I dedicate this book to all who are hurting from abuse, being, physically, mentally, or even spiritually.

Acknowledgements

I thank God for trusting me to be obedience to his voice. When he spoke and said it is time to release it.

Special thanks to my beloved late mom and dad Emma and David Wimberly for the love and the great sacrifices that was made for us.

I want to give a special acknowledgement to my publishing company WestBow and everyone that was involved from the start to the finish.

Thanks to all my family, and friends for encouraging me to release what God had given me.

To the Gray's, Murry's, Smith's, Stone's, Thunderbird's, and Wimberly's. Thanks for all your prayers, support, and encouragement.

Nancy Wimberly

Thanks to my grandchildren and friends for all the love and support.

Thanks to all the readers. A new mindset is in the horizon.

Who can find a Virtuous woman?
For her price is far above rubies.

—Proverbs 31:10 (KJV)

Introduction

Who can find a Virtuous woman?

For her price is far above rubies.

—Proverbs 31:10 (KJV)

This inspirational message is a blessing to be shared with everyone. It's a blessing to let you know that no matter where you are in this walk of life—no matter how you feel about yourself or how others feel about you—you are worth far more than rubies are, and they are of great value. The scripture where God describes that your price is well above the price of rubies lets you know that you are valuable to him and to yourself.

It is such a blessing to know that you were born with a purpose and destiny—that everything you go through in life is not about you but to help someone else who feels the same way as you do.

Remember that you are far more valuable than rubies.

My prayers are that whoever reads this book will be blessed by it.

This book is written for God's glory!

Know Your Worth

Who can find a Virtuous woman?
For her price is far above rubies.
—Proverbs 31:10 (KJV)

In life times of struggling—low self-esteem, being bullied, picked on, provoked to fight to adulthood, or abuse—can make you feel worthless. You have not necessarily grown up the way I did. But somewhere your life took a turn for the worst; you thought it was over and that there was no end to the way your life was going. I'm talking about knowing your worth. At some point it appeared there was no worth in me. Then suddenly you begin to hear this small voice say, "Be encouraged. This is not the end—only the beginning of a new chapter in your life."

Reflections started to appear and my thought pattern was all over the place. If I could've, would've, or should've became a part of my vocabulary. Instead of going forward I slipped backward. However, throughout it all I continued to hear that small voice saying, "Be encouraged." With tears flowing down my face, I heard the Lord say, "Daughter, lift your head." I looked in the mirror, looking like a hot mess, and said, "This is not the end; this is only the beginning."

I was awakened one night and the Lord said, "Know your worth; you are far more precious than rubies." So, I began to research about rubies. A ruby, according to Wikipedia, is a pink- to blood-red-colored gemstone. The first thing that came to my mind was the red blood of Jesus.

So, the Lord said, "Look up the value of a ruby." Rubies, according to what I read, are popular gems. They are exceptionally durable. The most expensive gems cost are over $100,000 per carat. The price Jesus paid for us on Calvary is far more than $100,000 a carat. We are worth more than we think for Jesus to lay down his life for us.

So, I began to look over my life when I did not feel pretty or was too small or too overweight or just not good enough. That small, still voice would say to me, "Daughter, you are beautifully and wonderfully made by me. I formed you in your mother's womb." I immediately got up and read Jeremiah 1:5 (NIV), which says, "Before I formed you in the womb, I knew you, before you were born, I set you apart. I appointed you as a prophet to the nations."

See, when we thought we were being picked on, God was setting us apart because we are peculiar people, some say strange. His Word says in 1 Peter 2:9 (NIV): "But you are a chosen people, a royal priesthood, a holy nation. God's special possession, that you may declare the praises of him who called you out of darkness into his wonderful light."

You are worth more than you know. It's time to stop feeling sorry for yourself and allowing people, places, and things to determine your worth.

Take a moment to stand up and shake yourself. Decree and declare the following: I am and shall be everything God has called me to be. I can do all things through Christ, who strengthens me.

Pick yourself up, dust yourself off, and get back in the race. The race is not given to the swift nor to the strong but to those who endure until the end. Quitting is not an option; it should not be in your vocabulary.

See, if we know that rubies are valuable gems and God says our price is more than rubies, then that's who you believe—that's who you can depend on to never let you down. People will fail you, but God will never fail you. He knows your flaws, your strengths, and your weaknesses.

So be encouraged and know your worth. You are beautifully and wonderfully made by him. You are the head and not the tail. You were bought with a price.

Know your worth! Know who God says you are. Walk into the fullness of God's potential for your life.

Reflections

1. How do you feel about yourself? Be honest.

Nancy Wimberly

2. What do you think people think about you? Be honest.

3. What was said or done that has you thinking the way that you do? Be honest.

Now let's take it all to God in prayer. First, ask for forgiveness of yourself and of anyone who may have spoken over your life or done things to you that harmed you physically, mentally, or even spiritually.

You are going to release it all to him.

Now second, let's give thanks. Thank him for keeping you and thank him that you are still here.

Start off with identifying the problem, then go to God with prayer and thanksgiving and begin to live instead of just exist.

Prayer

Forgiveness with Thankfulness

Dear heavenly Father,

Forgive me for not knowing my worth.

Forgive me for not believing in you about myself according to your Word (Psalm 139:14 NIV). I praise you because I am fearfully and wonderfully made; your works are wonderful—I know that full well.

Forgive me for when I felt all alone. Your Word says in Deuteronomy 31:6 (NIV): "Be strong and courageous. Do not be afraid or terrified because of them, for the LORD your God goes with you; he will never leave you nor forsake you."

Forgive me when I trusted in people and not you. For your Word says in Proverbs

3:5 (NIV): "Trust in the LORD with all your heart and lean not on your own understanding."

Forgive me when I was hard on myself because of what people said about my appearance. Your Word says in 1 Samuel 16:7 (NIV): "But the LORD said to Samuel, 'Do not consider his appearance or his height, for I have rejected him. The LORD does not look at the things people look at. People look at the outward appearance, but the LORD looks at the heart.'"

I ask you, heavenly Father, to come into my life and take over again or even for the first time. Be Lord over my life in everything I say or do. I come to you with thanksgiving in my heart and praises on my lips.

I release the pain of the past to you—words that were said or spoken over my life. I release my thoughts to you, for your Word says, "Finally, brothers and sisters, whatever is true, whatever is noble, whatever is right, whatever is pure, whatever is lovely, whatever is admirable—if anything is excellent or praiseworthy—think about such things" (Philippians 4:8 NIV).

Thank you, Father, for renewing my mind, for your Word says, "Do not conform to the pattern of this world, but be ye transformed by the renewing of your mind. Then you will be able to test and approve what God's will is—his good, pleasing and perfect will" (Romans 12:2 NV).

Thank you, Father, for being my deliverer. Your Word says in 2 Samuel 22:2 (NIV), "The LORD is my rock, my fortress and my deliverer."

Thank you, Father, for cleansing my heart, for your Word says, "Create in me a pure heart, O God, and renew a steadfast spirit within me" (Psalm 51:10 NIV).

Thank you, Father, for giving me peace during the storms, for your Word says "And the peace of God, which transcends all understanding, will guard your hearts and your minds in Christ Jesus" (Philippians 4:7 NIV).

Thank you, Father, for the times when I felt like the enemy was winning. Your Word says, "From the west, people will fear the name of the LORD, and from the rising of the sun, they will revere his glory. For he will come like a pent-up flood that the breath of the LORD drives along" (Isaiah 59:19 NIV).

Thank you, Father, for when I thought I was lost "your word is a lamp for my feet, a light on my path" (Psalm 119:105 NIV). In Jesus's name, amen.

Printed in the United States
By Bookmasters